Testimonies Of
Faith

Michele Ortega

ISBN 979-8-88685-325-4 (paperback)
ISBN 979-8-88685-326-1 (digital)

Christian Faith Publishing
832 Park Avenue
Meadville, PA 16335
www.christianfaithpublishing.com

Printed in the United States of America

Acknowledgments

The thought of writing this book first came to me in a dream for two consecutive nights. I am elated that this dream has become a reality. I give thanks and praise to Almighty God for his guidance so that I could successfully complete this project.

To my late husband, Dr. Emmanuel Ortega, thank you for your love, dedication, and support throughout our eighteen years of marriage. I miss you immensely and I thank you for making my dreams come true. May you rest in peace, my love.

I would like to acknowledge Audrey Seymour for her time spent with me in prayer, her knowledge, and her wisdom. This book would not have been possible without her support.

To my parents, Deonarine and Majorie Koopsammy, I thank you for your love and support throughout my life and for helping me to stay focused on the completion of this book during the many challenges of life.

To my "other parents," Roy Charles and the late Mary Charles, thanks for your love and sense of caring throughout the years.

To my brother, Dave Koopsammy, you are a one-in-a-million brother, and I thank you for always being there for me whenever I call on you.

To my aunts in Trinidad, I am truly blessed to have you all in my life, and I thank you for your sense of caring, love, and support.

To my pastor, Dr. Newton Hoilette, thank you for inspiring me and being my role model. Your spiritual guidance is paramount to me.

To my brothers and sisters of the Lehigh SDA Church, you all are very special to me, and I thank you all for your love and support throughout the years. To Dr. Georgette Hinds, thanks for your love, words of wisdom, and support. To Joycelyn Locke, Nadine Gordon, Susan Hamilton, Duval and Janet Ruddock, and Murline Bromfield, you are all gems and I thank you for your sense of caring and support always.

To Michael Deo, thank you for your prayers and support throughout the years.

To John Kelly, Michelle La Duke, and Theresa Winters, you have truly touched my heart with your kindness, and I thank you for going above and beyond to assist me when I needed your help.

To Percy T. Williams, you are such a unique and genuine individual. I thank you for your sense of caring, kindness, positivity, and wisdom throughout this project. You have been such an inspiration to me and I thank you for giving me words of encouragement on the days that I was faced with many challenges. You have been such a blessing in my life, and I appreciate you.

To Navin D. Ramsaran, you are such an amazing person and a loyal friend. Thank you for always being there for me when help is needed. I appreciate your sense of caring, support, and advice.

To Alvin Ramsaroop, you are such a talented individual. I thank you for being a genuine and loyal friend. Most of all, I thank you for always making me smile with your music and your sense of humor. I truly appreciate you.

To Jaime Rampersad, thank you for investing your time in the creation of the beautiful portrait photography that is illustrated in this book. Your work is outstanding and unique.

Finally, to everyone who invested their time and energy in the creation of this book, I thank you from the bottom of my heart. May God bless you always!

O give thanks unto the Lord; for he is
good; for his mercy endureth forever.

—1 Chronicles 16:34 (KJV)

Michele Ortega
I would love to hear from you! Feel free to email
me at testimoniesoffaith8@gmail.com to share your
thoughts and feedback after reading this publication.

Contents

My Mother, My Rock

My son, hear the instruction of thy father,
and forsake not the law of thy mother.

—Proverbs 1:8 (KJV)

According to the holy bible, a parent's role is to be a good steward to the children that God has put into their care. A parent's responsibility is to care for the emotional, spiritual, and physical well-being of their children. The most important biblical duty of a parent is to teach their children about Jesus Christ.

The knowledge of Jesus Christ is the best gift that I have ever received from my mother, Mrs. Majorie Koopsammy, and from the bottom of my heart, I would like to thank her for taking the time to educate me about God. It is this precious gift of introducing me to God that has made me stronger as a woman throughout the years, as I have learned to put my trust and faith in God whenever I am faced with life's challenges.

I can clearly recall having a conversation with my mom, and in that conversation, she told me that while she was pregnant with me, she would go down on her knees every day and pray to God. I responded by saying to her,

"No wonder I have a strong spiritual relationship with God. I was praying to him before I was even born." We both laughed at my response, but my mom has always been a faithful servant to God.

As far as I can recall during my childhood, my mom would wake us up every morning with gospel music. At the age of six, I had already learned the words of Jim Reeves's gospel songs such as "Take My Hand, Precious Lord," "This World Is Not My Home," and "I'd Rather Have Jesus," as my mom loved listening to Jim Reeves gospel music on a daily basis.

My parents were Catholics, and my mom made it her duty that every Sunday morning. Whether it was raining or the sun was shining, I had to wake up early in the morning to go to church. As a child, there were a few Sunday mornings that I really wanted to sleep in, and I tried to make excuses for not wanting to go to church. However, my mom did not fall for any of my excuses. She always told me that you have to put God first, and everything else will fall in place or work out for you in life. Therefore, I soon developed a love for God, the Catholic religion, and gospel music. I became very involved in the church as I joined the choir as a child and never missed choir practice on Saturdays. I enjoyed being in the choir and singing solo at times during mass on Sundays at church.

During my preparation for the sacrament of confirmation as a Catholic, I had the opportunity to go on a retreat for a weekend at Mount St. Benedict in Trinidad which allowed me to spend some time with a few nuns from the convent. I spent time in prayer for hours with these nuns during my retreat and I felt so happy and peaceful. It was such a beautiful experience that I came to the realization that the more time I spent with God in prayer, the closer I felt to God.

As a Catholic and a young adult, I had my first vision at church at the age of twenty-one. When I had my first vision, I did not know what was happening to me as I had never experienced it before, so I was a bit scared. I recalled telling my mom about my vision while we were leaving church one Sunday morning. I told her that while we were praying at church and my eyes were closed, I saw myself in the church dressed in black and white and standing in front of a brown coffin. However, when the coffin was opened, there was no one in it, and there was no one else in the church at the time besides myself. I told my mom that the vision lasted for a minute but seemed so real, and I opened my eyes pondering if someone was going to die in our family. My mom told me that she did not think that anyone was going to die in our family, so at that point, I just forgot about that experience. However, a few months later I realized the meaning of my first vision.

I began to face the challenges of life as I struggled to find a good job after graduating from the University of the West Indies: School of Continuing Studies, and I started drifting from my relationship with God by spending less time in prayer. Therefore, I realized that the vision signified that if I was not careful, my relationship with God would end. After a few months had passed, I realized that I needed to repent and spend more time in prayer in order to strengthen my relationship with God, and so I did. My family and I remained faithful Catholics for many years.

However, a few years later after spending time studying the bible and visiting an evangelistic meeting in the village, my mom decided to get baptized in the Adventist faith.

We all had questions in our minds as to why she wanted to choose this path as a Christian. However, my mom explained to me that she was being drawn to the evangelistic meetings in the village every night, and she felt that this was the fate that God was calling her to after she had a dream one night after praying to God. My mom got baptized into Adventism, and it was then that she experienced the power of God like never before.

I remembered visiting my mom's church in Trinidad while I was on vacation in the year 2014, and it was an experience that I would never forget. As I listened to the praise and worship part of the service, tears ran down my eyes, and I was drawn to Adventism and wanted to be baptized as soon as possible. A week later, I got baptized and became an Adventist and I felt the presence of the Holy Spirit like never before.

I was very happy with this decision and I continued to seek God and gain a closer relationship with him. It was then that I was able to experience the goodness and blessings of God like never before as God answered my prayers and gave me so many testimonies for me to share with you in this book.

Again, I had to thank my mom for introducing me to Adventism, for if she did not choose this path, I would not have chosen that either. As an Adventist, I gained knowledge about the bible as I often did bible study and began to attend sabbath school, so I was able to learn about God's laws, the

Ten Commandments. I started observing the sabbath by resting on the seventh day of the week and devoting time to worship and giving God praise on that day, and it made a difference in my life as God continued to bless me in many ways.

As a parent, you may not be able to give your child everything that your child desires. However, the gift of spirituality is one of the most precious gifts that you can give to your child because your child will use this gift throughout life and seek God when faced with challenges in order to survive in the world today. Thank you, Mrs. Majorie Koopsammy, for giving me this precious gift of spirituality, so that I can have daily conversations with God, and my faith can be strengthened as I grow closer to God.

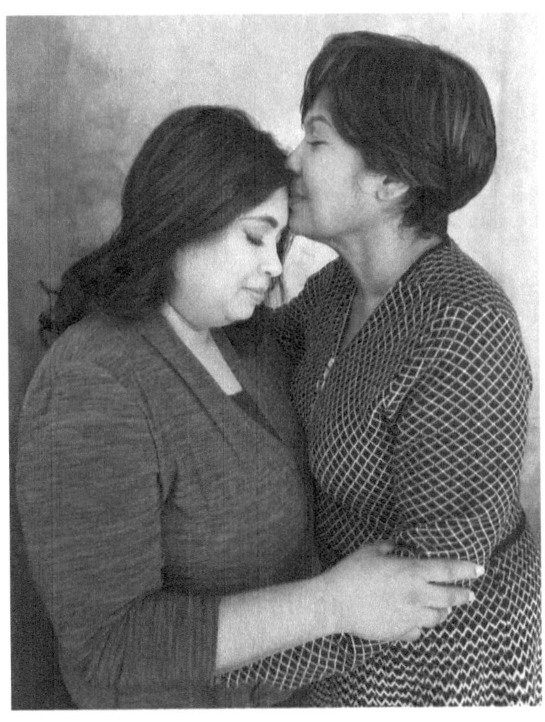

A Dream Comes True

For I know the thoughts that I think toward
you, saith the Lord, thoughts of peace, and
not of evil, to give you an expected end.

—Jeremiah 29:11 (KJV)

I can clearly recall during my childhood; it was always my greatest wish to visit the United States of America and make this beautiful country my home. I would go to school in Trinidad and hear interesting and exciting stories from my friends who had visited New York and Florida while they were on summer vacation. However, the opportunity never arose for me to visit this country, and I never thought that one day my dream would come true, and I would be residing in the United States of America.

As I grew from a child into an adult and entered the working world, employment opportunities for me in Trinidad seemed quite grim as I was only gaining employment with small private organizations that did not offer any benefits and paid very little. I honestly yearned for a change of environment and a new start in my life and, of course, for my dream of living in the USA to somehow come true.

In January 2001, I had finally given up on my dream of visiting the United States of America, and I felt heartbroken because it was something I really wanted. However, sometimes in life when you are about to give up on your prayers or your wish coming true, it is then that God opens up doors for you. *Ephesians 6:10(KJV) states, "Finally, my brethren, be strong in the Lord, and in the power of his might."*

In March of 2001, my mom coincidentally met her godmother, the late Mrs. Mary Charles, who resided in the USA for many years and was on vacation in Trinidad. My mom had not spoken to her godmother in years and was delighted to connect with her, so she invited Mrs. Mary Charles and her family to our home for dinner one day. Mrs. Charles and her family accepted the invitation and visited our home for dinner. It was at this time I met Mrs. Charles and felt an instant connection with her. She had a beautiful smile and a wonderful personality. She was extremely happy to meet me, and my mom mentioned to her that it was my wish to visit the USA and possibly make this country my home. As soon as Mrs. Charles heard that I wanted to visit the USA, she responded by telling my mom to send me to her home and that she would gladly take care of me. I was very shocked by her response as I had never met anyone in my life who was willing to welcome me to their home at such short notice. Mrs. Charles gave me hope and made me so happy with her response. I felt as though she was sent by God and was the answer to my prayers.

Therefore, in April 2001, I decided to apply for a visitors' visa for the USA, and I was very thankful and elated that I was given a ten-year visitors' visa. I began to make preparations for my first trip to the USA. This was the first time I was traveling internationally and by myself, so I was nervous and excited at the same time. I had decided that I was going to stay six months in Florida so that I could explore universities to further my education.

I left Trinidad in June 2001 to visit the USA, and Mrs. Charles and her spouse welcomed me with open arms at the Southwest Florida International Airport in Florida and brought me to their home. Their home was beautiful, and they did their best to make me feel at home and comfortable daily. I missed my parents, but Mrs. Charles and her spouse, Mr. Roy Charles, treated me so well and showered me with love that they soon earned the title of being called "my other parents."

One week after I arrived in Florida, I was surprised to discover that Mrs. Charles had enrolled me at Southwest Florida College so that I could pursue my associate's degree in information technology management. I was super excited and began to attend college. During my first semester, I was enrolled in three classes that were considered full-time, and I maintained an A grade in all my classes. After a month of attending college, I met Emmanuel Ortega who was one year ahead of me in college, and we became best friends. At the time, I did not know that this was the guy that would become my future husband.

I attended college for six months, and during this time, if I was not attending college or studying, Mrs. Charles and her family would take me sightseeing to various places in Florida. One of my favorite places that I was able to visit with Mrs. Charles and her spouse was Disney World. I was super happy to meet my favorite character, Mickey Mouse, at the Magic Kingdom theme park and I felt like a kid again. We visited all of the theme parks in a week, and I took lots of photos. I was thankful for this opportunity and enjoyed every moment with my new family.

Mrs. Charles took the time to teach me to drive and ensured that I got my driver's license so that I could drive to school at times. The six months that I spent in Florida went by so quickly, and December came and I was fortunate enough to spend Christmas with my new family before returning to Trinidad. I felt so loved because on Christmas Day as I entered my room, I saw so many presents from my new family. The tears came to my eyes, but they were tears of joy. Mrs. Charles and her family had definitely made a positive impact and difference in my life, and I felt sad because I knew that I had to return to Trinidad. However, Mrs. Charles told me that she knew that I would be back soon, and that brought a smile to my face. Mrs. Charles always seemed to make you feel better and put a smile on your face whenever you felt sad or were having a bad day.

I left Florida on December 28, 2001, and returned to Trinidad and was excited to see my family and tell them about my experience in Florida. My parents were happy that I had started school and was very thankful to Mrs. Charles and her family for all that they were doing for me. I had planned to continue my studies at Southwest Florida College. However, I could only do so if I had attained a student visa. Therefore, when I returned to Trinidad, I decided to apply for a student visa. I visited the US Embassy in

Trinidad with all my documents and was asked one question when I applied for my student visa. I was asked if I was already attending college, and I stated that I was attending Southwest Florida College. With that response, I was granted a student visa. I was in awe but elated at the same time because this meant that I could return to Florida, finish my studies, and spend time with my new family.

I returned to Florida in mid-January 2002 and continued with my education at Southwest Florida College and stayed with my new family. As the year progressed, I began to spend more time with Emmanuel, and from being best friends, the relationship progressed to the next level. Finally, one evening in December 2002 while I was in college, Emmanuel proposed to me and asked me to be his wife. I was very surprised but said yes to him. He was very happy with my response and wanted to get married as soon as possible. However, I had decided that I wanted to graduate before I got married. Therefore, we decided that our wedding would be held in Trinidad on July 13, 2003. This gave me enough time to plan my wedding, and Mrs. Charles assisted me with the wedding planning while my parents prepared their home in Trinidad for a wedding. Indeed, it was an exciting time for everyone. I graduated with honors in May 2003 and had a beautiful graduation ceremony. Mrs. Charles and her family attended the ceremony, and so did Emmanuel.

Emmanuel and I, along with Mr. and Mrs. Charles, flew to Trinidad at the beginning of July 2003 for our wedding. We had a beautiful wedding ceremony at Fatima RC Church in Trinidad and an awesome reception at my parents' home in Trinidad. We went to Barbados for our honeymoon and returned to Trinidad a few days later. Then it was time to leave Trinidad and return to Florida at the end of July 2003. I felt sad leaving my parents in Trinidad, but I had grown to love my life in Florida. I said goodbye to my family in Trinidad and traveled back to Florida with my new family and my husband, Emmanuel.

When I returned to Florida, I realized that it was time for me to start a new life with Emmanuel, and this meant leaving the home of Mr. and Mrs. Charles. This was a sad moment for me. However, Mrs. Charles reminded me that we could visit her home as much as we wanted. Therefore, Emmanuel and I started living in an apartment, and one year later, we moved into our new home. I got a job with a renowned retailer and decided to continue my education, so I began to pursue my bachelor's degree in management. I continued to excel in my studies and at my job. As a result, I was promoted several times at this retailer and loved my job as I was working in my field of study which was management.

We visited Mr. and Mrs. Charles often, and they were both very happy and proud of my accomplishments, and so were my parents in Trinidad. I was very thankful that my dream had become reality as I was now residing in the USA. I never knew that this would happen, but indeed God had answered my prayers, and I am thankful to God for his many blessings to me. He made a way for me when I thought it was impossible. I have been residing in the USA for almost twenty-one years, and this country has become my home as I eventually became a US citizen through naturalization. At times, I miss my family in Trinidad, but living in Florida has enabled me to accomplish so many great things that seemed impossible in Trinidad.

Indeed, the USA is the land of opportunities; however, one of the greatest opportunities that we are all given as human beings is the opportunity to develop a relationship with God. Once you seek God and accept him in your life, he will be your guide throughout your life, and you will accomplish great things, so choose God today. *Philippians 4:13 (KJV) states that "I can do all things through Christ which strengtheneth me."*

Could This Be an Angel
who Rescued Me?

I will lift up mine eyes unto the hills, from
whence cometh my help. My help cometh from
the LORD, which made heaven and earth.

—Psalm 121:1–2 (KJV)

I was driving to work on October 19, 2015, at approximately 10:30 a.m. and I began to contemplate what a beautiful day it was as the sun was shining brightly and I could see the clear blue skies from a distance. The clear blue skies brought a smile to my face, and I thought about what a wonderful day it was going to be. As I looked to my left, I could see a couple who was in a minivan waving at me. It seemed as though they were trying to get my attention for some reason. They tried talking to me from their vehicle, but I could not hear what they were saying to me. I decided to bring the glass on the door of my car down, so I could hear what they were trying to tell me. The couple slowed down so that they could communicate with me and so did I.

Apparently, the couple observed that I was driving with a flat tire and wanted to let me know. As soon as they told me that the back tire on the left side of my car was flat, they drove off. I did not even get a chance to thank them for communicating this piece of news to me. Upon hearing this news, I decided to stop at the side of the road and take a look at the flat tire. As soon as I got out of my car, a guy who was driving another car slowed down and started yelling to me, "There is a gas station a few minutes away. Drive to the gas station, and you will find someone who can help you with that flat tire." After yelling at me, the guy also quickly drove off.

At that point, I started to think about how I was going to resolve this problem. I told myself that I was not going to drive to the gas station with a flat tire, but at the same time, I knew that I clearly did not know how to change a flat tire. Additionally, getting a flat tire on the road while driving had always been one of my fears, and I started to get nervous and scared. I looked at the tire, and it was then that I remembered that I had a tire inflator in the trunk of my car. Therefore, I decided to open the trunk and utilize the tire inflator to inflate the tire. After trying three times to inflate the tire, I realized that I was just wasting my time. I did not know whether I was not using the tire inflator correctly, or if the tire was so flat that the tire inflator was inappropriate for this situation.

I decided to put the tire inflator back in my trunk as I began to feel frustrated. I thought about calling my husband to come and rescue me. He was at work at the time, and I really did not want to bother him. Additionally, it would have taken him an hour and a half to get to my location, and I had to be at work within an hour, so it did not make sense to contact him.

It was at that moment I went inside my car and I decided to pray. I began to speak to Jesus and I told him that I had a flat tire and I did not know how to change it. I begged him to please send someone to help me as I was a bit scared and concerned that I would reach work late. I also thanked him for his many blessings to me and for always answering my prayers. After praying, I got out of my car and decided to open the trunk and check for a spare tire. As I was about to close the trunk, I looked to my left and I saw this African American gentleman with dreadlocks dressed in a milky white tuxedo and wearing sparkling white shoes approaching me with a smile. I was in awe and a bit scared as well as I did not know him. The gentleman looked at me and smiled and told me that he saw that I had a flat tire, so he stopped to change the tire for me. I immediately responded to him by saying, "Oh, thank you so much. I am truly grateful for your help."

It was then that I opened the car trunk and took out a rug and spread it on the road for the gentleman. I told him that I was going to get him another rug so that his white tuxedo would not become soiled. However, he told me that he would be fine and proceeded to lie down on the rug to change the tire. I assisted him by giving him the tools that were needed to change the tire, and in ten minutes, he changed the tire.

The gentleman then stood on his feet, and I proceeded to put the tools in the trunk. As he was about to leave, I thanked him again for his help and I asked him if I could please have his name and mailing address so that I could mail him a gift card as a thank-you present. The gentleman hesitated to give me his information, but I asked for his information one more time. He then told me his name and his address, and I wrote them down so that I could mail him a gift card. I then told him it was nice to meet him and thanked him for his kindness. He began to walk on the pavement, and I proceeded to go inside my car. However, when I looked to see if he was still walking on the pavement, he was no longer there.

This felt so strange to me, and I was surprised. I asked myself where could he have gone as I did not see him driving a vehicle. It seemed as though he had just disappeared in seconds, but how could this be possible, I asked myself? I was unable to answer my question, so I closed my eyes and thanked God for sending someone to assist me in my time of need. God had once again answered my prayers. I pondered for a moment after praying if it was possible that God sent an angel my way. However, I could not confirm if this was an angel, so I simply said out loud, "God, I know it was you who sent someone. You are amazing, and I thank you, Lord."

With a smile on my face, I continued to drive my car and arrived to work on time. I purchased a gift card and thank-you card for this gentleman who had assisted me with the flat tire. I signed the card, wrote a quick thank you note, and mailed the card to the gentleman. However, one week after, the mail was returned to my home with a note stating that the address was not found. I then located the piece of paper with the information which I had written and verified that I had written the correct information on the envelope. It was evident that the information was correct, so I could not comprehend the reason why the mail was returned to me. At that point, I told myself that I would just let this go and not worry about this situation anymore because at the end of it all, God knew that I meant well and was truly thankful for the help which I received.

Saved from an Accident

God is our refuge and strength, a
very present help in trouble.

—Psalm 46:1 (KJV)

Most people who reside in Lee County in Florida are familiar with State Road 82 as it is a twenty-nine-mile-long east-west highway that serves Northern Lee and Collier County in Florida. The popular State Road 82 is frequently used by hundreds of people every day, and it was also part of my commute when I worked in Naples in the year 2019.

On February 4, 2019, at approximately 6:35 a.m., I was driving on State Road 82 as I was on my way to work in Naples. Every day I would drive forty-eight miles one way to get to work. Therefore, I would listen to gospel music while driving as it was quite relaxing, uplifting, and inspirational.

While I was driving on busy State Road 82 on this particular morning, I recalled receiving a text from my brother. It was unusual for my brother to text me that early in the morning, so I thought to myself, maybe this was an important text from my brother. As I was about to pick up my phone which was very close to me, I felt a sudden jolt from the car as it made a quick swerve to the right. As soon as this occurred, I tried to straighten the car and steer it to the left. However, once again it made another swerve to the right, and even though I made another attempt to straighten the car by steering it to left, it seemed as though I was losing control of the car as I was unable to steer the car in the direction I wanted it to go.

It was at this point I felt scared and decided to let go of the steering wheel since I did not know what else to do. I remembered saying, "Jesus help me" when I let go of the steering wheel, and the car made a complete circle three times in the middle of State Road 82. As the car was going around in circles, I could hear loud noises as if I had hit other vehicles and I began to tremble. The thought of my vehicle getting in an accident and hitting several vehicles made me quiver and I closed my eyes and thought that this was going to be the end of me. Honestly, I felt as if I was going to die. Then suddenly, I realized the car was turned off. I opened my eyes and realized that I was still in the car but the car was no longer on State Road 82.

The car was parked on an empty piece of land which was located on the left side of State Road 82, and the ignition was off. After a few minutes had passed and even though I was still scared, I decided to open the door and come out of the car so that I could view the exterior of the car. However, as I opened the car and tried to put my feet on the ground, I discovered that there was mud, and I did not want to get mud on my shoes. At this point, I closed the door and decided to turn the ignition of the car on to see if it would start.

The car started as if it was in perfect condition, and I heard this inner voice telling me to get back on the road and drive to work. I thought for a moment and asked myself if I should drive to work or if I should go home. However, again I heard that inner voice telling me to get back on the road and go to work. Therefore, I decided to do so.

I started to drive at thirty-five miles per hour as soon as I got on the road because I wanted to be cautious since I was not sure if everything was really all right with the car. However, the car seemed to be working well, so I increased my speed to forty-five miles per hour. As I drove to work, I was still concerned about how the exterior of the car was looking since I did not come out of my vehicle to look at it. However, I continued to drive and made it to work forty minutes later.

As soon as I parked my vehicle at work, I sat in my car and closed my eyes and thanked God that I had arrived to work safely, and I also prayed to God for the vehicle to be in a good condition. Then I opened the door and came out of the car. I could see mud on the tires of the car, and as I walked around the car, tears came to my eyes as I realized that my car did not have any damage, dents, or scrapes. There was a bit of grass that was trapped in the rims of the tires and mud on every tire.

At this point, I became so emotional and started crying as I was amazed at what God had done for me. He saved me from an accident. I was alive, and nothing was wrong with my car. I kept saying, "Thank you, God" as I proceeded to walk to my office. I quickly dried the tears from my eyes as I saw one of my employees approaching me. As my employee greeted me, I began to narrate to her what had happened to me that morning, and she listened attentively to my testimony. When I was finished telling her about my testimony, she stated that she was truly touched by my experience. She stated that she was a Christian and believed in Jesus Christ and attended church every week. She then proclaimed that God is an amazing God, and we both proceeded to begin our work for that day.

In times of trouble always remember Isaiah 41:10 (KJV), which states "fear thou not; for I am with thee: be not dismayed; for I am thy God: I will strengthen thee; yea, I will help thee; yea, I will uphold thee with the right hand of my righteousness."

A Miracle from God

Save me, O God; for the waters are come in unto my
soul. I sink in deep mire, where there is no standing:
I am come into deep waters, where the floods
overflow me. I am weary of my crying: my throat
is dried: mine eyes fail while I wait for my God.

—Psalm 69:1–3 (KJV)

The year 2015 would always be a memorable year for me as I experienced God's power like never before. In October 2015, my husband, Emmanuel, who was employed as the program services director of a medical institution in Southwest Florida, started experiencing symptoms such as shortness of breath, lack of sleep at night, chest pain, bloating, weight gain, and water retention which required medical attention. He decided to visit his primary care doctor who quickly referred him to a cardiologist.

After one visit to his cardiologist, he was ordered to immediately check in to the emergency room at Lee Memorial Hospital in Fort Myers, Florida. Emmanuel reported to the emergency room the same day, and they started running tests on him. His weight had increased immensely during the month of October due to water retention, and this was a big concern for the medical staff at Lee Memorial Hospital as they gave him medication to reduce the retention of fluid in his body.

After three days of extensive testing at Lee Memorial Hospital, Emmanuel was diagnosed with congestive heart failure, and he was advised by his cardiologist that he needed to be transferred to Gulf Coast Medical Center, Fort Myers, as it was mandatory that he had to undergo surgery so that they could put a defibrillator in his heart since his heart function was abnormal at the time.

On the fourth day of Emmanuel's hospitalization, he was transferred to Gulf Coast Medical Center and was scheduled for surgery. On the day of Emmanuel's surgery, I stood by his side as he seemed brave and ready for surgery, but at the same time, he was concerned if he would make it through the surgery. The time came when the medical staff took him to the operating room, and I was all alone in the waiting room which seemed very cold at that moment. The only person I had with me at the time was God, so I closed my eyes and prayed throughout his surgery. I also reached out to my pastor, Dr. Newton Hoilette, and informed him about Emmanuel's situation. He prayed with me over the phone and told me that he, along with my church family, would be praying for Emmanuel. After three hours of being in the waiting room alone, the cardiologist told me that Emmanuel was very lucky as he had almost died during surgery, but they were able to save him, and the surgery was successful.

I was able to see Emmanuel forty-five minutes after surgery, and he seemed to be very tired and in pain. They moved him to a room in the hospital since he was going to be there for a few days recovering from surgery. At 6:30 p.m., my pastor, Dr. Newton Hoilette, visited Emmanuel in the hospital. He was just as concerned as I was since Emmanuel was not looking too well after surgery. My Pastor prayed with Emmanuel, and then he told me that I should try and get some rest since I had a very long day. I then said goodbye to Emmanuel and left for home as I had planned to visit him the next day. My church family at Lehigh SDA church, his family, friends, my parents, and the members of my mother's church in Trinidad continued to pray for Emmanuel daily.

When I came home, the house felt so empty as I had been alone at home for the past four days and I was a bit worried about Emmanuel as he had just undergone surgery. I prayed that he would have a speedy recovery. The next day I visited Emmanuel in the hospital, and I was very surprised to see that he was wearing a sleep mask and was hooked up to oxygen as he continued to experience shortness of breath. He struggled to keep the mask on and would unconsciously pull it off whenever he was awakened from his sleep. The medical staff would express their frustration to me about the challenges they faced daily with him since he could not keep the mask on his face as it was very uncomfortable for him. Eventually, he asked the nurse to please tie his hands down, so he would not remove the mask. I was very thankful that the nurse did not do that as they thought that was too harsh for him.

The medical staff worked with Emmanuel to locate a mask that was more comfortable for him, and he eventually obtained one that was much more comfortable. However, he began retaining fluid in his body again, and even though the medical staff had prescribed different medications for him, nothing seemed to be able to reduce the amount of fluid in his body.

After, six days of being at Gulf Coast Medical Center, I received a call early one Saturday morning from Emmanuel. He had called me to tell me that the cardiologist had told him that he was going to die and he wanted to see me before he died. At that point, I told him that I would be there as soon as I could and immediately rushed to get dressed to go to the hospital. As I was driving, I called my parents in Trinidad and told them what was going on. They were very concerned, but at the same time, they were thousands of miles away from me. Tears started running down my eyes as I continued to drive to the hospital, and I prayed to God for a safe arrival since I was experiencing so many emotions at the same time. I was scared, anxious, and extremely sad all at the same time.

When I arrived at the hospital, the cardiologist spoke to me and told me that Emmanuel had seven days to live as his body was not responding to any of the medication that was being ministered to him. Therefore, they were going to transfer him to hospice where he would comfortably spend his final days. I was devastated. The thought of Emmanuel dying at the time was very overwhelming for me.

After the cardiologist spoke to me, the nurse came and gave us both a hug as both Emmanuel and I were in tears. As they prepared him to be transferred to hospice, the entire medical team came into the hallway to say goodbye to him.

This indeed was the saddest day of my life. As they placed him in the ambulance, I went to my car as I was instructed to drive behind the ambulance.

As I sat in my car, I received a call from my mom from Trinidad who had Pastor Beckles and his wife with her, and Pastor Beckles was concerned about how Emmanuel and I were doing. I then relayed the sad news to Pastor Beckles; however, to my surprise, Pastor Beckles responded by saying that he had an urge to pray with me on the phone, and so he did. My tears went away, and Pastor Beckles told me that he firmly believed that this was not the end for Emmanuel. Pastor Beckles gave me hope, but as I began to drive to hospice, I kept thinking about what the cardiologist had told me. I prayed to God for strength, as I really was not prepared for Emmanuel's death.

We arrived at hospice, and Emmanuel was given a very comfortable room at hospice. I met the nurse, and she explained to me that they would do everything in their power to make Emmanuel as comfortable as possible in his last days, and they would focus on pain management at hospice. She then asked me what religion I belonged to, and I told her that I was a Seventh-day Adventist. She was very happy with my response and encouraged me to explore the dietary options that Seventh-day Adventists use as she believed that a change in diet for Emmanuel would prolong his life. I thanked her for her advice and then said goodbye to Emmanuel as it had been another long day for both of us, and it was time for him to get some rest.

I had chosen to send Emmanuel to a hospice location in Cape Coral, Florida, since I worked in Cape Coral,

Florida, at that time. The next day I visited Emmanuel at hospice, and even though he had a nice room, he seemed uncomfortable as he was still retaining lots of fluid and was unable to sleep comfortably. Emmanuel stayed at hospice for approximately two weeks. I would visit him twice daily during this time because on the days that I worked, I would spend my entire lunch hour with him; and then after work, I would stop by and spend time with him before going home. He was always very sad when I was leaving to go home and begged me to spend one night with him at hospice.

Even though I was scared to spend a night at hospice, I realized it was one of Emmanuel's wishes, so I spent a night with him. Honestly, it felt really strange spending a night at hospice as there were many sick people and you could hear their cries at night, so I was very happy to leave when the morning came.

While Emmanuel stayed at hospice and the days passed by, I began to notice that he always seemed to be unaware of his environment and did not seem to recognize his friends and family who visited him daily. There were days that I would talk to him, and he would seem so lost or as if he was in a different world and did not understand what I was saying. I could not comprehend what was going on with him and I thought to myself that maybe his health was deteriorating.

At the end of Emmanuel's two-week stay at hospice, I was notified by hospice that they were going to send Emmanuel home as a home hospice patient since his health was not improving, and they would send a nurse to visit him once a week to see how he was doing. I was devastated and really worried because I had no one who could take care of him at home, and I was working full-time. After all, the bills needed to be paid, so I could not stop working.

Upon hearing the news that Emmanuel was coming home the next day, I recalled praying in the little office of our home for hours. I cried out to God like never before to help me as I was all alone. I begged God to please send someone to help me. I remember while praying, tears kept running from my eyes, and the song "Hear, O Lord, the sound of my call" was playing. I tried to sing along, but I was crying so much that I could not sing, and I prayed and cried until I had no more tears left. I eventually slept away on the desk of the office in our home.

The next morning my mom called and to my surprise, she told me that she was going to come and visit me and spend a month with me to help me take care of Emmanuel. God had answered my prayers by sending my mom to help. The next day, Emmanuel came home, and the master bedroom was set up just like a hospital room as he was given a hospital bed and oxygen tanks. This was where he was going to spend his last days according to hospice. At this point, Emmanuel was home but still appeared to be in his own world as he was totally unaware of his environment.

A nurse from hospice took the time to inform me about his medication and at what times it should be given to him. Emmanuel was taking nine different prescription medications at the time. It was then that I discovered that one of the medications that Emmanuel was taking was morphine for pain management, and I did not have a good feeling about morphine. There was this inner voice that seemed to be talking to me and was telling me, *Do not give Emmanuel any morphine*. I could not understand why, so I decided to follow my mind.

My mom arrived the next day, and I was elated to see her. Just having my mom with me gave me hope and comfort. She was going to be a caretaker for Emmanuel while I was at work, and she did a great job. My mom has always been a firm believer in alternative medicine, and as soon as she came, she began to tell me that she was going to change his diet. She was going to put Emmanuel on a special diet which consisted of homemade soups and the juicing of fruits and vegetables. I informed my mom about Emmanuel's medication so that she would be able to give him his medication daily. My mom had a daily routine that she would consistently follow. Every morning she would pray with Emmanuel before she prepared his meals, and on the days that I was off from work, we would all pray together.

Whilst Emmanuel was a home hospice patient, Pastor Dr. Newton Hoilette, the members of the Lehigh SDA church, members of my mom's church, friends, coworkers of Emmanuel, and I and our families all prayed consistently for Emmanuel's recovery and healing and visited Emmanuel at home.

After the first week of my mom staying with us, we began to see a bit of progress with Emmanuel as he was now aware of his surroundings. I noticed that since we had stopped giving him morphine, he was fully aware of his environment and was now able to recognize everyone and was able to have a good conversation with his visitors. The change in his diet also helped as he was able to eat comfortably without feeling bloated, and he looked forward to my mom's daily cooking. It was indeed a joy to have my mom around. Emmanuel's nurse from hospice began to visit him and was happy with the progress he had made.

After the end of the second week of having my mom with us, Emmanuel began to walk around the house comfortably with his oxygen. He expressed his desire to go outside as he had not been outdoors in weeks, so we decided to let him spend a few minutes outdoors one day. He came back inside with a smile on his face as he became so emotional and stated how wonderful it felt to feel the sunshine on his skin.

Emmanuel then began to spend more time outdoors as the days went by, and there were two ladies from Lehigh SDA who would visit Emmanuel weekly and do bible study with Emmanuel. He really enjoyed having these ladies around and spending his time doing bible study.

Then one morning approximately one month after Emmanuel was sent home from hospice, we sat down for our morning devotion and prayed together. When our prayers were completed, Emmanuel went to his room and removed his oxygen and came out to the living room and told my mom and me that he was going to take a walk outside. We were both in shock, and I asked him where was he going to go without his oxygen, and he stated to me that he did not need it anymore. My mom and I started to wonder what was going on.

I followed Emmanuel outside and observed him walking on the lawn and enjoying the fresh air that he was now able to breathe. He said to me, "Michele, I feel great! I can breathe, I can run, and I can walk and I am going to be okay because God has given me another chance." It was at that point I realized that God had answered our prayers. Emmanuel had received a miracle, and we were all elated.

Emmanuel's nurse visited him later that week and was in awe at his progress, especially since he did not need oxygen. She spent time talking to my mom and asked her what type of diet she put Emmanuel on, and my mom stated that it was mainly fresh soups, fruit, and vegetable juices. We all knew that it was more than Emmanuel's diet. It was also divine intervention.

We thanked our Pastor, church family, immediate family, friends, and coworkers for their continued prayers and support, and they were all happy to hear the wonderful news about Emmanuel. On the Saturday of that week, we all went to church and we gave God thanks for his goodness. Our Pastor, Dr. Newton Hoilette, gave Emmanuel a special welcome back to church and mentioned to the congregation Emmanuel's journey over the past few months, and he gave God praise and thanks for answering all our prayers for Emmanuel.

Emmanuel scheduled an appointment to see his cardiologist the next week and was given clearance to return to work. His cardiologist was baffled to see such progress but was very happy for Emmanuel. Two weeks later, Emmanuel returned to work, and his coworkers welcomed him with open arms. Emmanuel told his testimony of God's goodness to him for many weeks as people were confused as to how he had recovered from being so ill. Emmanuel did not hesitate to tell everyone that it was all God's work and gave God all the praise and glory.

"Now unto him that is able to do exceeding abundantly above all that we ask or think, according to the power that worketh in us. Unto him be glory in the church by Christ Jesus throughout all ages, world without end, A-men" (Ephesians 3:20–21 KJV).

Hurricane Irma

For thou hast delivered my soul from death, mine
eyes from tears, and my feet from falling. I will
walk before the Lord in the land of the living.

—Psalm 116: 8–9 (KJV)

As a working individual, I would always plan to take a vacation at least twice a year. I enjoyed traveling, so during my vacation, I would always plan to visit Trinidad and Tobago or another country or state within the United States of America. However, when it came to selecting the dates for my vacation, I would always pray about it to seek God's guidance.

I had always wanted to take my parents on a vacation to a place that they would really enjoy, one which they would have never thought that they would visit in their lifetime. Therefore, in the year 2017, I decided that I was going to take my parents to Hawaii for a vacation. I chose Hawaii because it was on my bucket list of places that I desired to visit in my lifetime due to its beautiful beaches and culture.

In August 2017 I called my parents and asked them if they would like to go on a vacation with me to Hawaii. They both got really excited at the thought of visiting

Hawaii. However, even though my dad loved the thought of going on vacation to Hawaii, due to the nature and demand of his business in Trinidad, it was impossible at that time of year for him to go on a vacation. Therefore, my mom decided that she would go with me and Emmanuel to Oahu, Hawaii, and I bought tickets for our trip without hesitation. Emmanuel had spent eight years in Hawaii, so he was very excited to visit Hawaii once more.

My mom arrived in Florida on August 23, 2017, and we left for Hawaii on August 28, 2017. We had planned to spend sixteen days in Hawaii. We had to take a connecting flight to get to Hawaii which meant that we had to travel from Fort Myers to Texas and then take another flight from Texas to Oahu, Hawaii.

Texas and Louisiana were hit by Hurricane Harvey on August 25, 2017, which was a devastating category four hurricane that caused catastrophic flooding and many deaths. Therefore, as we approached Texas just before landing, we could see the flooding and devastation in Texas, and we all felt very sad and heartbroken for the people of Texas.

After arriving at the airport in Houston, Texas, we quickly embarked on the next flight from Houston, Texas, to Oahu, Hawaii, which was an eight-hour flight. Since Hawaii was six hours behind Florida, we arrived in Oahu, Hawaii, at approximately 4:00 p.m. on August 28, 2017. Upon arriving at the airport in Hawaii, we were immediately impressed with the Hawaiian people as they seemed very helpful, warm, and friendly.

I had made reservations at a hotel that was located exactly three miles from Waikiki Beach in Hawaii. This hotel had complimentary transportation for everyone who was staying at their hotel. We were all able to relax and enjoy the scenery and the ride from the airport to the hotel. We soon realized that Hawaii reminded us of the islands in the Caribbean, and we were really amazed at the huge beautiful mountains in Hawaii.

We arrived at the hotel within forty minutes and settled into our beautiful suite. We then decided to go for a walk, do some shopping, and have dinner. We discovered that we could walk to Waikiki Beach since it was only ten minutes away, and so we would walk to the beach every day. We admired the trolleys daily as Hawaiians utilized these trolleys as a means of transportation. We selected an amazing tour guide who presented us with leis, took us around the island, and told us amazing stories about his experiences as an actor, surfer, and resident of Hawaii.

We visited the Polynesian Cultural Center, Pearl Harbor, beautiful beaches, malls, flea markets, and Dole Plantation. One week had passed by, and we enjoyed every minute of being in Hawaii. We enjoyed the sound of the live saxophone player every night which we could hear from the balcony of our hotel and tasted unusual vegetarian dishes which we loved. Additionally, we enjoyed a fresh cup of chai tea from Kona Coffee at International Market Place most mornings, and being in Hawaii felt like we were truly living in paradise.

Then on September 8, 2017, we heard the news that Hurricane Irma was going to hit Florida as a category four storm, and I began to worry. We were away from our home, and there was no way that we could prepare our home for a hurricane, so this news definitely changed the mood of our vacation. Then I had to remind myself that God was in control and that I had to let go and let God. "Casting all your care upon him; for he careth for you" (1 Peter 5:7 KJV).

Hurricane Irma eventually hit Southwest Florida on September 10, 2017, as a category four hurricane. I can recall sitting in our hotel room and looking at a video of the devastation and flooding where we lived in Florida. Suddenly, I just wanted to return home as I began to think about the possibility of our home being destroyed. Emmanuel and my mom reminded me that I needed to have faith. Emmanuel was able to contact a friend who checked on our home and told him that we had some roof damage to our home, but the damage did not need any immediate attention. I was relieved to hear this news and thankful to God that at least our home was still standing.

I also decided to check the status of our flights since we were scheduled to leave Hawaii on September 12, 2017. I was not surprised when I discovered that all flights to Florida were canceled. This meant that we would have to extend our vacation in Hawaii for another week.

At that point, I went into a bit of a panic mode as I was concerned about my job and being away from it for so long. Then I started to contemplate if the hotel would allow us to stay for an extra week and when were we going to get a flight back home. I immediately spoke to God and pleaded to him to help me with this situation.

A few minutes later, I decided to go to the reception area of the hotel so that I could speak to one of the receptionists. I mentioned to the receptionist that our flight was canceled due to a hurricane in the area in which we lived, and immediately the receptionist responded by saying that she heard about that hurricane and she was so sorry to hear that it had hit our area. I then proceeded to ask her if we could stay another week in our current suite and she responded by saying, "Of course!" She also told me that she would give us a fifty percent discount for that week due to the circumstances, and I was so grateful for her help.

Then I decided to call the airlines to see when exactly we would be able to return home, and in minutes, I was given a flight that coincided with our extended hotel stay. This really made me feel so much better, and I then decided to notify my employer that I was stuck in Hawaii for one more week. Well, to my surprise, I discovered that my employer was totally fine with that and told me that our place of work suffered some damage to the building and was awaiting repairs, so extending my vacation for another week was fine. Indeed, I was very thankful to God for working everything out for us. "In every thing give thanks: for this is the will of God in Christ Jesus concerning you" (1 Thessalonians 5:18 KJV).

Since everything worked out so well and my mind was at peace, we decided to go for a walk along Waikiki beach that afternoon. There were many vendors along the beach, and while we were walking, a female vendor from Israel stopped me to ask me, "Where did you reside?"

I responded by saying, "We live in Florida." As soon as she heard my response, she then asked me if we lived where Hurricane Irma had made landfall. I responded by saying "yes," and at that moment, she gave me a hug and told me that if we were to return home and did not have a place to live, she would be happy to take us into her home and ensure that we had food to eat. I thanked her for being so kindhearted and empathetic toward us as she had really touched our hearts with her words. We then continued walking along the beach, and I started to think to myself that I was really happy to know that there were still some good people left in the world.

We enjoyed our last few days in Hawaii, and on September 19, 2017, we left Oahu, Hawaii, for Fort Myers, Florida. After we arrived at Fort Myers International Airport, we took a minibus to get to our car, and the driver of the bus started to talk about his experience with Hurricane Irma. The driver stated that he would never stay in Florida for another hurricane because experiencing Hurricane Irma was very scary for him and his family.

He then proceeded to tell us that his home suffered a lot of roof damage and he lost a lot of furniture from the flooding. Additionally, he also stated that he did not have any electricity or water at his home and he had no idea when he would be getting electricity since thousands of people were without water and electricity. I asked him where did he live, and to my surprise, I discovered that he lived in Lehigh Acres, the same city that we lived in.

I then began to worry because I started to ponder the possibility of us not having electricity or water as well, but soon reminded myself that no matter the situation, God would take care of us. We then got into our car, and Emmanuel began to drive to our home. We were all astonished as we noticed the destruction of our city from Hurricane Irma. We could see buildings totally destroyed, power lines, trees, and street signs lying on the side of the road, and many businesses were closed. It was really sad and devastating because it would take months to restore the damage that was done by Hurricane Irma.

We soon arrived home and discovered that some of our landscaping was destroyed and we had some roof damage to our home. Our neighbor told us that he did not have electricity or water and that all the residents in Lehigh Acres did not have electricity or water either. Upon hearing that, as soon as we entered our home, I turned on the light switch to see if we had electricity, and I was so happy to discover that we had electricity and we also had water. Immediately, I said, "Thank you, Lord, you always take care of your children!"

Our house required a new roof, and we were concerned that we may have to pay thousands of dollars for the roof. However, we were lucky that our insurance company covered the entire cost of the roof so that we got a brand-new roof for our home without having to pay any money out of pocket. God took care of our needs! God is awesome!

"And even to your old age I am he; and even to hoar hairs will I carry you: I have made, and I will bear; even I will carry, and will deliver you" (Isaiah 46:4 KJV).

God Restored My Health

And ye shall serve the Lord your God, and he
shall bless thy bread, and thy water; and I will
take sickness away from the midst of thee.

—Exodus 23:25 (KJV)

On Sunday, January 19, 2019, at 7:00 a.m., I woke up
with a sharp chest pain that I had never experienced
before as I tried to get off the bed. As I felt this pain, I
decided to lie down for a few minutes to see if the pain
would somehow vanish. It had been a very tough month
at work as I had been working sixty-five-hour weeks and I
was dealing with a high level of stress in the workplace. I
tossed and turned on the bed, and the more I moved, the
more I felt the sharp pain in my chest. I decided to get up
from the bed and take a couple of aspirins to prevent any
possible heart attacks.

After taking two aspirins, I decided to get dressed to
go to work since I was the only manager on duty that day.
Twenty minutes after taking the aspirins, the chest pain had
decreased, and I left to go to work. While driving, I thought
to myself that if the chest pain did not go away completely,

I would call a supervisor to come in, and I would go to the emergency room to seek medical attention.

I arrived at work and started my normal routine. However, two hours later, I felt the chest pain increase again. So I decided to call a supervisor to come in and work for me so that I could go to the emergency room. At 1:00 p.m. I left work and drove to Lehigh Regional Medical Center since that was the closest hospital in the vicinity of my home.

I was fortunate that as soon as I arrived and the nurse heard that I was having chest pain, they began to check my blood pressure and perform an electrocardiogram (EKG) on me. After reviewing the results of the EKG, they gave me six aspirins to swallow as they stated that they had observed some abnormal activity. I began to get scared and concerned as this was turning out to be more serious than I thought it was going to be, and somehow, I got the feeling that I would be admitted to the hospital. I started to pray and asked God to please help me and calm my fears. "These things I have spoken unto you, that in me ye might have peace. In the world ye shall have tribulation: but be of good cheer; I have overcome the world" (John 16:33 KJV).

The nurse then proceeded to take a couple of blood tests and after four hours of being in the emergency room, I was given the news that I was going to be admitted to the hospital as they had planned to perform an echocardiogram on me the next day. They also decided to give me cholesterol medication as they stated that my cholesterol was elevated. Indeed, this was a surprise to me because as far as I knew, I did not have any health issues in my life.

Somehow, nothing made any sense to me because I would always complete a full medical checkup twice per year and I was never diagnosed with high blood pressure, high cholesterol, or any other medical issues. I was also a vegetarian and tried to maintain a healthy diet. I continued to pray about my situation because all I wanted to do was feel better and be able to go home. I decided to inform my boss that I was in the hospital and was unable to go to work for a few days. At the same time, I ensured that my shifts were covered at work while I was at the hospital.

Half an hour later, I was admitted to the hospital and I was thankful that I had a room for myself. However, I felt so alone and scared because I had never been in the hospital before. As the night approached, I looked forward to getting some rest. However, this seemed impossible as every two hours, the nurse had to take blood tests and give me aspirins. I was definitely not a fan of taking prescription medication, nor did I ever enjoy seeing blood or needles, so it was very painful for me to endure these blood tests so often.

The next day at around 10:00 a.m., they performed an echocardiogram and a chest X-ray on me. After the cardiologist reviewed the results of the echocardiogram, he stated that my results were very rare and abnormal. He stated that in all his years of being a cardiologist, he had never seen any abnormal results such as mine and he could not determine what exactly was going on with me. He recommended further testing and instructed the medical team to treat me for possible blood clots as a preventative measure.

Upon hearing this news, I decided to reach out to my church family to let them know what was going on with me because I needed additional prayers. My church family began to visit me in the hospital and pray with me, and through it all, Emmanuel also spent as much time with me as possible. The additional support and prayers helped a lot because I began to feel that I was not alone and that I was lucky to have so many people who truly cared for me. I told myself that I needed to have more faith and trust in God because the God that I serve had never failed me.

> Jesus answered and said unto them, "Verily I say unto you, if ye have faith, and doubt not, ye shall not only do this which is done to the fig tree, but also if ye shall say unto this mountain, be thou removed, and be thou cast into the sea; it shall be done. And all things, whatsoever ye shall ask in prayer, believing, ye shall receive." (Matthew 21:21–22 KJV)

On Tuesday morning, a male nurse came to give me my aspirins and also took blood tests. However, he was very gentle with the needles, and I thanked him for taking his time drawing blood. He viewed my chart and told me that he wanted to talk to me. He then proceeded to close the door and knelt down at the side of the bed. He then asked me what was going on with me in a very soft tone, and I told him that I was admitted to the hospital due to chest pain and that I had a very stressful job and was dealing with a high amount of stress during the past month.

I told him that I truly believed that the stress was having a negative impact on my health. He then told me that he agreed. He had been through a divorce six months ago and had extreme chest pain during his divorce and also ended up in the hospital. He stated that he had always been a healthy person and that he knew that the level of stress he endured during his divorce was the cause of his chest pain. He informed me that after his divorce was finalized, the chest pain went away. He then mentioned to me that if the hospital were to suggest to me that I needed to undergo a heart catheterization to let them know that I did not want to complete that procedure as it was not necessary. I thanked him for his advice, and he left my room.

As he left the room, I got this feeling that this male nurse genuinely cared for me and that somehow God had used him to give me this message. Well, an hour later, the cardiologist came to see me and told me that they were going to transfer me to Gulf Coast Medical Center in Fort Myers because I was in need of heart catheterization, and that was the only hospital that had the facilities for that procedure. The cardiologist emphasized that since most of my tests showed abnormal results, heart catheterization was imperative so that the medical team would be able to figure out what was really going on with my heart. I told the cardiologist that I understood what he was saying, but somehow, I was a bit skeptical about this procedure.

Later that evening, I was transported by an ambulance to Gulf Coast Medical Center and I was placed in a room with another female patient. I felt tired and I was looking forward to a good night's rest. However, again I was unable to get much rest due to the blood tests that had to be taken every two hours.

On Wednesday morning, the cardiologist visited me and told me that on Thursday they were planning to schedule me for a heart catheterization. I immediately asked the cardiologist if there was any way another test could be conducted instead of heart catheterization since this was an invasive procedure, and I did not feel comfortable with this procedure. The cardiologist stated that he could send me for a couple of stress tests later on in the day, and if the stress tests had good results, then they would cancel the heart catheterization. I told him that I would appreciate that very much, so I was scheduled for two stress tests later that Wednesday.

At approximately 2:00 p.m. on Wednesday, I had an exercise stress test and then a nuclear stress test. I can recall the technician telling me that I had done the right thing by telling the cardiologist that I did not feel comfortable with a heart catheterization as it was not needed based on my medical history.

After taking both the exercise stress test and the nuclear stress test, I was very happy to know that the results for both tests were normal. As a result, the cardiologist stated that he would not recommend heart catheterization at this time and was willing to send me home the next day on one condition. He stated that I had to be scheduled for a CT (Coronary Angiogram) in a couple of weeks since this test would allow them to look at the arteries that supply blood to my heart and were often used to diagnose the cause of chest pain. I agreed to get this done and scheduled this procedure for a week later. I was told that the test would be a two-part exam, so I began to mentally prepare for this procedure by being positive and continuing to put my faith and trust in God.

A week later, Emmanuel accompanied me for the first part of the test, which included a detailed review of my medical history, blood work, and monitoring of my heart rhythm. The technician who was conducting the first part of the test asked me what was my profession, and I responded by saying that I was the general manager of a retail company. He quickly responded by saying that in the history of his career, he noticed that my profession was one of the professions that causes these symptoms in patients. I must say that I was seriously concerned and a bit scared after he mentioned that to me. However, I had to tell myself that God is a miracle worker, the greatest physician, and nothing is impossible with God. After the first part of this test was completed, Emmanuel and I left for the day, and we were told that I had to return the next day for the second part of the test.

The next day, Emmanuel accompanied me again for part two of the CT. The technician put me to relax in a reclining chair while they monitored my vitals, and an IV was placed in my arm. I was then moved to the CT table so that the technician could begin the CT scan. The CT scan was conducted, and I was told that I would receive the results two weeks later.

Two weeks later, I visited the cardiologist for the results of the CT, and I was told that nothing was wrong with my heart. He stated that I just needed to focus on managing my stress better due to the nature of my job. After receiving this news from the cardiologist, I was so relieved and immediately said, "Thank you, Lord." This was just another answered prayer from God.

"And Jesus said unto them, because of your unbelief: for verily I say unto you, if ye have faith as a grain of mustard seed, ye shall say unto this mountain, remove hence to yonder place; and it shall remove; and nothing shall be impossible unto you" (Matthew 17:20 KJV).

The Loss of a Legend

And God shall wipe away all tears from their
eyes; and there shall be no more death, neither
sorrow, nor crying, neither shall there be any more
pain: for the former things are passed away.

—Revelation 21:4 (KJV)

On New Year's Eve, December 31, 2020, my spouse, Dr. Emmanuel Ortega, was rushed to the hospital in our neighborhood because he was experiencing difficulty with breathing. Additionally, he was feeling unusually tired even when he was resting. The hospital stated that he would have to be admitted because they wanted to test him for COVID-19, so we both welcomed the new year at the hospital.

After two days of testing at the hospital, we were told that his COVID-19 tests were negative and that he was fine, so he was released from the hospital. During the month of January, Emmanuel was fine. However, in mid-February, he started having the same symptoms of being consistently tired and having difficulty breathing. Therefore, on February 15, 2021, I decided to take my spouse to the emergency room at Gulf Coast Medical Center in Fort Myers.

When we arrived at the hospital, we noticed that there were many patients awaiting medical attention as COVID-19 was on the rise during this time. This time instead of admitting Emmanuel to the hospital, they did some blood work and tested him for COVID-19. The COVID-19 test was negative again, and once again, he was told that nothing was wrong with him and he was sent home.

Since Emmanuel continued to have the same symptoms, he decided to consult with his cardiologist who suggested that he should be scheduled for a heart catheterization to determine if he had any underlying heart issues. The heart catheterization was scheduled for March 10, 2021.

Emmanuel and I woke up at 5:00 a.m. on March 10, 2021, and spent some time in prayer before leaving for the hospital for his heart catheterization. The procedure was supposed to be approximately forty minutes, and the recovery time was estimated to be one week. While Emmanuel was in with the cardiologist, I got down on my knees and prayed for the procedure to go well and that we would receive good results.

After approximately two hours, I was told that I could take Emmanuel home and I was thankful to God that the procedure went well. His cardiologist informed us that his heart was in good shape and recommended that he should schedule an appointment with a lung specialist if he continued to experience the same symptoms.

Emmanuel and I were both thankful that everything was fine with his heart, and we gave God praise for answering our prayers. However, Emmanuel continued to have the same symptoms as he was recovering from the heart catheterization. He attempted to schedule an appointment with a lung specialist, but was told that he had to wait six weeks for an appointment. Then on March 15, 2021, Emmanuel started to cough up blood and his oxygen level dropped to eighty-nine percent.

At this time, I told Emmanuel that I was going to take him to the hospital in our neighborhood because I was really concerned about him. This time I asked the medical staff to please do extensive testing because his symptoms were getting worse, and we needed to know what was really wrong with him. The medical staff admitted Emmanuel to the hospital and took another COVID-19 test, and once again, the result was negative. They then decided to take some blood tests and on March 17, 2021, we were told that Emmanuel had developed a blood clot in his lungs. The hospital treated him for the blood clot and told me that Emmanuel needed to be transferred to Gulf Coast in Fort Myers for further testing as he needed to be treated by a hematologist since he was identified with a blood disorder.

On March 18, 2021, Emmanuel was transferred to Gulf Coast Medical Center, and the medical staff again did extensive testing on him. Finally on March 19, 2021, at 11:00 a.m., I received a call from the hematologist at Gulf Coast Medical Center who had reviewed the results of Emmanuel's blood work, and I was told that Emmanuel was diagnosed with acute myeloid leukemia in the blood. I was also told that Emmanuel needed to be transferred to Tampa General Hospital right away so that he could be treated for this type of leukemia and that they needed to do a blood transfusion on Emmanuel right away.

This was shocking and devastating news for me. I immediately left the house and drove to the hospital so that I could see my spouse. My heart went out to Emmanuel, and I just wanted to be there for him as much as I could. I prayed while I was driving to the hospital because I needed strength to deal with this situation, and God was the only one that could assist Emmanuel with his medical diagnosis.

When I arrived at the hospital and came to Emmanuel's room, they were getting ready to move him to ICU. Emmanuel tried to talk to me as much as possible, but since he was having more difficulty breathing, it was very difficult for him to converse with me. Everything seemed to be happening so quickly. I was in shock, and not to mention, I was further surprised that the medical staff told me that he needed to go to ICU as soon as possible.

I became really emotional and started crying. Emmanuel felt the need to comfort me even though he was critically ill. At that moment, I felt scared that I was going to lose Emmanuel. The medical staff told both of us that whatever we needed to say to each other, it was imperative that we did, so at that time, that is exactly what we did.

I stayed at Emmanuel's side for as long as visiting hours allowed, and then I left to go home. Again, I prayed for strength because I could not help but think about Emmanuel's pain and suffering at that time. As soon as I pulled up in the driveway at home, I saw Emmanuel's vehicle, and tears started flowing from my eyes. I ran to the bathroom and looked in the mirror and started thinking about living in the house without Emmanuel, and I started screaming, "No, this cannot be happening, not Emmanuel!"

I sank to the bathroom floor, and my tears continued to flow until I had no more tears left. I then heard this voice telling me, "Michele, you need to be strong. You will get through this, and everything will be fine." I stood up and decided to take a shower and go to bed as I felt mentally exhausted from the day's events.

I woke up on Saturday, March 20, 2021, at 6:00 a.m., thinking about Emmanuel being in the hospital, and I had a ton of questions running through my mind. However, the main question that concerned me was how long did Emmanuel have this disease. At that point I decided to get up, shower, get dressed, and go visit Emmanuel. Saturday was always a day of rest for Emmanuel and me as it was the sabbath and also the day to spend time praying, praising, and worshiping God. Therefore, as I was driving to the hospital, I told myself that even though Emmanuel was in the hospital, we would both listen to our church service online and make God a priority.

As I walked into Emmanuel's room in intensive care, he saw me and he had the biggest smile on his face. He then told me that he was going to miss me and that he loved me very much. Even though I was emotional and sad, I had to be strong for Emmanuel. So I responded by saying, "Where are you going?" He then responded by saying that he did not think he was going to make it. It was at that point I told him that today being the sabbath, we are not going to be sad. I told Emmanuel that we were going to spend this day together giving thanks to God for all his blessings to us and we were going to enjoy this day with each other. Emmanuel and I talked, laughed, took photos together, and then we looked at our virtual church service.

After our church service, Emmanuel stated to me that he missed our Pastor and his church family and he wanted to create a few videos for the people he really loved so that these people would know how much he appreciated them. These were the people who were really there for Emmanuel when he really needed support. As Emmanuel began to create these videos, his oxygen level began to decrease, which made it difficult for him to speak. However, Emmanuel was persistent, and even though it was a challenge for him, he did not give up until the videos were completed. As he was creating the video for Pastor, his oxygen level dropped significantly and he started to cough, so it was at that point that I told him it was time to rest. Emmanuel fell asleep in minutes.

I stood there and stared at Emmanuel as he was asleep. I held his hand and started to pray for him, and I could feel the warmth of his hand. I prayed to God that he would either heal him or not let him suffer as I could not bear to see Emmanuel in pain and suffering. When he awoke from his sleep, he then sent these videos to the respective recipients from his cell phone, and they were all surprised and became emotional when they received them.

I enjoyed spending time with Emmanuel and I was there for him if he needed anything. At this point, Emmanuel could not leave the bed as he had to conserve his energy and oxygen as much as possible. Therefore, the hospital medical staff and I tried our best to make Emmanuel as comfortable as possible. He could no longer eat or even drink any liquids, and this really broke my heart. It is heartbreaking when you are with your loved one in the hospital and they ask for water or food and they are unable to eat or drink.

As I spent time with Emmanuel, whenever I felt like I was going to cry, I stepped out of the room and wiped my tears before I came back in. I did not want Emmanuel to see me crying. He eventually figured out that I was sad and confessed to me that he really hated leaving me and was worried if I would be okay without him. My immediate response was that God would take care of me. He always does. Emmanuel then told me that I was the wife he always wanted and that he wished he could give me so much more because I deserved it. It was at that point I started crying, and I told Emmanuel that I loved him and I would be there for him until the end. He thanked me for taking such good care of him, and I asked Emmanuel if he was ready to see Jesus. Emmanuel smiled and said yes. At that moment, as painful as it felt to possibly lose my husband, I was at peace because I knew that Emmanuel was ready to see Jesus. It was the end of another day, and once again, I had to go home. I felt sad leaving Emmanuel, and when I got home, the house felt so empty without Emmanuel.

On Sunday, March 21, 2021, I visited Emmanuel in the hospital, and he was sedated so that he could rest. He did not even know that I was there. I held his hand and prayed for him, and after I prayed for him, I felt like something had left my body. I had never experienced this before and I was shocked, so I sat down in the chair in Emmanuel's ICU room in the hospital wondering what had just happened to me. However, I realized that at that moment, I did not feel as close to Emmanuel anymore. It was at that point that I realized that this was a sign that Emmanuel was going to leave me, and I started crying and left the hospital.

Later that evening, they had decided to insert a breathing tube in Emmanuel to conserve his oxygen level, and he was faced with the decision if he should allow them to do that, or if he should just face death. It was then he reached out to our Pastor as he needed that reassurance from his Pastor that he was making the right decision by continuing to fight. Emmanuel got the opportunity to speak to both Pastor and me before they placed the breathing tube in him. He was given reassurance from our Pastor that he was doing the right thing by fighting until the end.

This was the last conversation Pastor and I had with Emmanuel, and Emmanuel did not hesitate to thank Pastor for his love and support. This was the last time that Emmanuel told me he loved me and he was going to be strong and fight this disease. I assured him that we would all continue to pray for him, and I told him to keep holding on to God.

On Monday, March 22, 2021, I visited Emmanuel in ICU, and he did not even know that I was there. Pastor came and anointed him, and we all continued to pray for Emmanuel. As Emmanuel's wife, I could not bear to see my husband in this state. He was suffering and in so much pain. I pleaded with the doctors to give him the best treatment, and they assured me that he was getting the best treatment. I consistently cried out to God to please heal him or not let him suffer because I could not bear to see his suffering. I left the hospital with tears in my eyes, and as I was walking down the hall, I heard a ringtone from my phone which was for an email. As I opened the email, I discovered that it was an invitation for an interview for a job that I had recently applied for, and it was a job that I always wanted. The interview was scheduled for Friday, March 26, 2021, and I accepted the invitation. As I approached my car, I thought to myself that God was so amazing, He knew that I was sad and he sent me this email to put a smile on my face. At that moment, the tears stopped flowing, and I was able to drive home safely.

Later in the day, I got the news that Emmanuel was going to be transported to Tampa General Hospital as soon as a bed was available so that he could be treated for acute myeloid leukemia. On Tuesday, March 23, 2021, Emmanuel was transported to Tampa General Hospital. He arrived at Tampa General Hospital at 7:15 p.m., and throughout the night, the hospital kept calling me with updates on Emmanuel.

I had planned to leave home early in the morning to drive to Tampa as the hospital recommended that I should visit Emmanuel in the afternoon. He was scheduled for testing on the morning of Wednesday, March 24, 2021. After his testing, I would be able to meet with a team of oncologists to discuss his treatment plan.

I woke up at 5:00 a.m. on Wednesday, March 24, 2021, and started to read the devotion for that day from my devotional book. I felt sick to my stomach after I was finished reading it, as the message in the devotional was to let go of loved ones, and I got the feeling Emmanuel was going to die. As soon as I was finished saying my prayers, my mom called me and stated to me that she had just read her devotional and said her prayers and she believed that Emmanuel was not going to make it. What a coincidence!

The hospital took Emmanuel for his tests that morning, and I began to have mechanical issues with my car that morning, so I had to visit the mechanic before leaving for Tampa. At 2:00 p.m. the doctor called me and told me that I should come quickly as Emmanuel was not going to make it. I told the doctor that it would take me four hours to get there since I did not live in Tampa and I would be there as soon as I could. I did not receive my car from the mechanic until 3:00 p.m. that day, so there was no way I could make it to Tampa in the time frame the doctor wanted me to be there.

At 3:30 p.m. the doctor called me and gave me the news that Emmanuel had just died and that he had a very peaceful look on his face. He stated that I needed to come to Tampa to sign off on his body, and I stated that I would be there by 8:00 p.m. When I came off the phone with the doctor, I had to sit down for a moment as I felt like my entire world had just been turned upside down. This was it; I was alone. I was now a widow. My family resided in Trinidad, and due to COVID-19 restrictions, they could not travel, so I had to be strong and make the necessary funeral arrangements by myself.

I started to make calls to let everyone know that Emmanuel had died. I called my pastor and my parents in Trinidad first. My Pastor was very concerned and insisted that I should not drive to Tampa alone. Therefore, Dr.

Georgette Hinds accompanied me. It was a pleasure having her around me as I considered her to be one of the mothers in my life. She did a great job comforting me during this difficult time.

We arrived at Tampa General Hospital at 8:00 p.m. and we were able to see Emmanuel. As I looked at his body, I could tell that he had experienced a lot of suffering. His body was cold, and it really hit me that he was dead. I completed the necessary paperwork and then left the hospital. Dr. Georgette Hinds and I spent the night at a hotel in Tampa as it had been a long day. Our plan was to leave the next morning to return to Fort Myers.

It was a rough night; I did get some sleep, but I felt this deep pain in my stomach that I had never felt before. I was in the physical stage of grief. We drove back to Fort Myers, and as I arrived home, my pastor, Dr. Newton Hoilette. greeted me and I was happy to see him.

Pastor and my church family prayed with me that evening for strength and comfort, and then I checked my email and realized that there was a follow-up email for me to complete an assessment for the job interview the next day. The deadline for the assessment was midnight, so I went online and started the assessment. It was a tough assessment, but to my amazement, in my mental state, I passed the assessment with a score of one hundred percent and then went to bed.

I woke up on Friday, March 26, 2021, and went to the job interview. When I arrived, the panel had heard the news of the death of my spouse. They extended their condolence and asked if I wanted to reschedule the interview due to the circumstances. However, I decided that I was going to continue with the interview, and I was interviewed by the panel and got the job. I was happy to receive the news and I was scheduled to start my new job in two weeks. However, I felt sad that Emmanuel was not alive to hear the good news because he would have been so happy.

Later that day, I met with the funeral agency to make funeral arrangements. God really was with me, giving me the strength to complete these tasks by myself. My church family really supported me during this time. On the days that I did not feel like eating, my church family would bring me food to ensure that I had something to eat. I had flowers coming to my house when I felt sad, and my church family kept praying for me and gave me moral and financial support. It seemed as though every need that I had during this difficult time was fulfilled by my church family.

Emmanuel was cremated a week after he passed away. A private viewing with family members was arranged prior to the cremation as that was exactly what Emmanuel wanted. This day was very rough for me as I looked at Emmanuel lying dead with his cold body. I often wondered why people would scream at funerals when they lost their loved ones. However, as I looked at Emmanuel lying dead, I started screaming uncontrollably. The pain one experiences after you lose a loved one is terrible, and having to deal with grief is something I wish that no one would ever have to experience in a lifetime. However, it is a part of life, and at some time we all will experience it.

Emmanuel's memorial service was scheduled a month after his cremation as it entailed a lot of planning. I needed time to plan because I was working full-time and also needed to coordinate with my pastor and church family. The memorial service turned out to be a beautiful church service with military honors, and his ashes were placed to rest at the end of the service. This was a tough day for me, and when I got home that day, it was tough being at home as the house felt so empty without Emmanuel.

Grief is one of the deepest pains anyone can experience. You never get over the loss of a loved one. You just learn to live without them because you have no other choice but to do so. There are times that I have flashbacks of Emmanuel, his suffering, and his death, and I burst out in tears. It is during these times that I go down on my knees and I pray to God for strength. My faith and trust in God have helped me with the loss of Emmanuel, for God gives me the strength to go on and continues to bless me daily.

Though I miss my husband immensely, I am thankful for eighteen years of marriage, and I will cherish our memories forever. Dr. Emmanuel David Ortega has left a legacy behind and has definitely made a positive impact throughout the world with martial arts. I consider myself very fortunate to have been married to a legend.

"Oh, how great is thy goodness, which thou hast laid up for them that fear thee; which thou hast wrought for them that trust in thee before the sons of men" (Psalm 31:19 KJV)!

God Is Alive!

The Lord liveth; and blessed be my rock; and
let the God of my salvation be exalted.

—Psalm 18:46 (KJV)

On Monday, April 4, 2022, at approximately 5:45 p.m., I was looking forward to going home as I had an extremely busy day at work. I had a headache and felt mentally exhausted from working all day, so I felt a sense of relief when I sat in my car and began to drive out of the employee parking lot at work.

As I was driving along Martin Luther King Boulevard in Fort Myers, a heavy shower of rain started falling, and I started thinking to myself, *where did this rain come from?* it did not look as though it was going to rain. Suddenly the rain started pouring even heavier, and in minutes the road was flooded with water, so I had to drive at twenty-five miles per hour. I could barely see the road because my surroundings looked white as the rain was falling so heavily. This was scary for me as I always disliked driving through the rain especially when I could hardly see anything.

At that point, I decided to drive at twenty miles per hour and put my emergency lights on as I did not want to get in any accidents due to the weather. Suddenly, I heard a loud noise as though something had fallen on my car, and I jumped. For a minute I began to think that maybe something was mechanically wrong with my car, as I was not driving a new vehicle. However, I continued to drive, and then I heard the same loud noise two more times. I looked at the windshield of my vehicle and saw a huge block of ice, and it was then I realized that it was haling.

The hail started pounding on the vehicle, and it was then that I started to pray because I could not see the road. The road was also flooded, and due to the location where I was driving, there was no way to stop and park or even pull aside, so I had to continue driving. I prayed to God to reach home safely and to allow the rain to slow down since I was having a difficult time driving. I pleaded to God to please answer my prayer as I just wanted to reach home safely, and after praying for five minutes, the rain started to slow down, and I was able to see the road better. I also prayed to God for it to stop hailing as I was concerned that my car would be damaged in some way with the large blocks of ice consistently falling.

It is always amazing to see that when you sincerely turn to God in your time of need and are faithful to God and his commandments, he answers your prayer. After a few minutes of praying for the hail to stop falling, the hail stopped and the rain eased up immensely. I felt so relieved and said, "Thank you, Jesus!" Immediately, I thought to myself, *God is not dead. He is very much alive and he is such a faithful God.*

Finally, I arrived home at approximately 7:00 p.m. and sat on the sofa for a few minutes. I closed my eyes and thanked God for his goodness to me and for being such a faithful God.

"I will speak of the glorious honour of thy majesty, and of thy wondrous works. And men shall speak of the might of thy terrible acts: and I will declare thy greatness" (Psalm 145:5–6 KJV).

O praise the LORD, all ye nations:
praise him, all ye people.
For his merciful kindness is great toward us: and
the truth of the Lord endureth for ever.
Praise ye the LORD.

—Psalm 117 (KJV)

Conclusion

And the Lord, he it is that doth go before thee;
he will be with thee, he will not fail thee, neither
forsake thee: fear not, neither be dismayed.

—Deuteronomy 31:8 (KJV)

All praise, honor, and glory be to Almighty God for his goodness to me and my deceased spouse, Dr. Emmanuel David Ortega. Indeed, I am elated that I am able to testify about God's goodness to us in this book. I pray that it may touch the lives of many people, give you hope, and increase your faith in our Lord.

We live in a world where we are faced with many problems and challenges daily, and it is of utmost importance to make God a priority, seek him, and stay focused on him because we need Him more than ever to help us get through each day. One day we can be wealthy people, and the next day we can be homeless. We are faced with many disasters in the world today, and so many people are suffering and ill. We need God in our lives.

I began writing this book in the year 2020, and from the time I began to write, I have been faced with the most challenges I have ever faced in my life. At one point, I did not think that I would ever complete this book as my problems were overwhelming at times. I resigned from a job I loved due to circumstances beyond my control, I was unemployed for almost a year, and was a caretaker for my spouse at the same time of unemployment. Finally, I lost my spouse due to death in March 2021. Additionally, I lost a couple of friends and members of my church family in 2021. However, through my many challenges, I diligently prayed to God, stayed faithful to his commandments, and trusted that he would answer my prayers and provide solutions for my problems and challenges.

God gave me strength when I was weak and hope when I felt like I could not go anymore. He provided for all my needs, and I am truly thankful to God for his many blessings. I urge you to please be faithful to God's commandments, believe in him, and make him a priority in your life. Talk to God, let him know your needs and your problems, seek his forgiveness for your sins, repent, and he will answer your prayers and work things out for you. As God answers your prayers, your faith will increase, and you will learn to depend on God more than before. May God bless you and your family richly.

About the Author

Michele Ortega was born on the beautiful island of Trinidad and Tobago. She migrated to the USA in 2001 and currently resides in Florida. As a child, Michele always had a special love for God and often attended church with her family. Her faith in God increased throughout the years as she held on to God during the many trials and challenges of life. It is through these trials that she has learned to make God a priority in her life as she has seen God giving her strength to face each challenge, answering her prayers, and pouring his blessings upon her life. Michele's personal testimonies have been an inspiration for many who seek God. She enjoys listening to music, traveling, and spending time with her friends and family in her free time. Michele's favorite scripture is "I can do all things through Christ which strengtheneth me" (Philippians 4:13 KJV).